*To everyone reading this     you for taking time out of    purged truly from my sou       ...    too scared to verbally express      ...ngs I need you all to know so that you can grasp understandings of life, love and happiness that took me so much pain and loss to ever understand. There are never particular answers for the things we go through but there are always ways we can cope and overcome them, I hope that you find something here which benefits your growth and prosperity in the most positive way possible.*

*To my dearest mother, the woman who gave me life and shown me how to find my way even in the midst of complete darkness. You would always tell me that the world is my oyster and anything I want I can have, you probably don't know how powerful your love and your commitment to me has been as my mother and my best-friend but I will forever be indebted to you and promise that if I do one thing in this life it is to never stop making you proud.*

Love Always.

*Metanoia;*

*The journey of changing your mind, heart, self or way of life.*

*Trials & Tribulations*

[ Firstly, I want to congratulate you on getting through all the trials and tribulations you have experienced in life thus far, you may not have known it at the time but it was those same things that are the reasoning behind your true purpose in life. Even I found this hard to believe, how can so much loss, hurt and despair be the path that leads towards me achieving what is meant for me but here I am.

There is something outrageously amazing about you, even if you don't know it yet.

Your answer lays within you and the strengths you have displayed throughout your life, there are never any instructions on how to overcome the things we go through although others may experience similar, they are not able to get into our mind and our being. You know exactly how you survived, if you are still learning how to I would like you to know that your divine purpose is waiting for you and if you take the time to evaluate the details around your bad experiences you will find a way to deal with them too.

Is there a person causing them that you can get rid of or is it just that life has handed you an unfair card?

All of the trials and tribulations you have faced in the past have been ones you've found your way out of but I bet at the time there seemed to be no end to the bad feelings you felt. It is completely normal and no your problems are not less troubling than anyone else's just because theirs may seem like the end of the world, yours may feel like they are too. Remember that the bad we face could never compare to the happiness and joy we can feel if we work on gaining a better understanding of our life and our-self, when we do this we are able to view these bad times as phases that will pass instead of moments in time we feel stuck in.

It is easy to sink so deep in the negative that we lose sight of ever finding the positives again.]

## <u>Keysha's domestic abuse</u>

I had lived a very ordinary life with very few to little problems as a child, besides growing up with a bad relationship regarding my biological father I was somewhat so a very happy child. School was never an issue and I excelled until reaching my teen years, this is when I can recall problems starting to arise. Growing up I was quite chubby and not the prettiest but once I had reached elder years I met new friends and moved up the rankings in a new school, I was suddenly someone people wanted to avoid there were barriers people didn't want to cross with me and I had the power to do what I wanted to do. There was very little that phased me now because if it did I would bully my way out of it, it wasn't long before I was skipping school to jump trains and getting into stealing, fighting and losing interest in my education. Prior to these years I never really had much interest in boyfriends and this remained for a while. Relationships were very empty and meaningless to me, my lack of relationship with my dad turned me off of it, I didn't really understand the big deal.

When I did meet someone he was very similar to the things I did know about my dad and it was that which interested me, there was something unusual about him which I wanted to know more and more about. I was infatuated with him. It was exciting knowing he was a distraction but thinking I could most probably make it right if I really wanted too. I was still fairly young and anything prior to this was just meaningless fun so I wasn't very experienced in the relationship department, he was eager to help me become a matured woman as soon as he got his hands on me.

The relationship didn't start off by giving any bad signs or red flags, like many I was tricked; the devil was once an angel after all. I feel as though it had begun with great innocence with very little intention of it being potentially as serious as it turned into because I didn't have much experience, it wasn't a matter of months either more a matter of weeks before I found myself putting education aside so that I could make more visits to be with him, he was something new and new always makes you want more. I wasn't a virgin but it seemed different with him as though it was a lot more serious and we would share what I assumed was passionate and intimate moments. He soon asked for me to spend more and more time around him, I was addicted to the feeling of being wanted and although I knew he was distancing me from reality it seemed like the better option.

Weeks would pass and I would be with him for each one, some nights we stayed up for hours just talking and getting to know each other, other times he would take me out to dinner then run me a bath when we got in. Sat on the toilet seat, he would tell me how beautiful I was and when he wrapped me in the towel he made the effort to kiss all the parts of my body I would moan about. It was different but it made me feel good. At the time he was involved in illegal forms of making money so it was as though he had all the time in the world for me. I didn't ever think ahead, in a way I figured that life had been determined for me and that was where I was destined to be so nothing else really mattered. He played a very good game and managed to work his way through everyone in my life quickly and convinced me that nobody wanted good for us. My friends didn't really agree with the relationship because it was distracting me from my own life, I would stupidly tell him how they felt and fuel his fire to dislike them even more. In all honesty I just thought maybe they were jealous because I was seeing someone and it was more serious than their relationships, never did I think they could see things that I was blind to.

Everything was roses and dinner dates for a while but things between us began to deteriorate by the fourth month and he started acting very possessive, always demanding to look through my phone and if I refused he would snatch it out of my hand and lock himself in the bathroom for hours on end just because he knew how much it annoyed me. Whenever I asked why he would just say it is for my own good because he wanted to protect me from people who didn't like him, I think my lack of fatherly love lead me into believing that for the first time a man cared enough to look after me. I couldn't have been more wrong. A little part of me knew that this possessive side to him was frightening, people were becoming aware of us being an item now and I was starting to hear rumours about him from his previous relationship with his child's mother. Some people had mentioned to a friend of mine that he had beaten her and was arrested, a little part of me believed it but a bigger part of me didn't want to so I put it to the back of my mind and tried to ignore it.

There came a time I anticipated knowing whether or not it was true and I decided to consult him on what I had heard. Even mentioning it angered him, I saw a change in his eyes they seemed to darken and cloud over me as though I had said something really vile. The whole idea of me daring to question him infuriated him, he flew from one side of the room towards me like a raging bull pulling me by my shoulders, shaking me back and forth screaming in such a fast lip motion that he was spitting foam into my eyes. Accusing me of believing her and suggesting I was going to tell people, he pushed me down onto the sofa. Silence echoed throughout the whole room and everything seemed black and white, I stared at the ceiling with absolutely nothing in my mind it was just silence and darkness. Not a single thought and fear of even daring to move a muscle in case that made him mad too. He came storming into the room with a beer in one hand and his other hand out in my reach as though he wanted to help me up.

This was the first time he viciously placed his hands on me, the way he had gripped me by my shoulders, forcing his fingers into my skin leaving red imprints and a purple finger bruise. I was in shock and really thought it was my fault.
Why didn't I just keep my mouth shut?
Why did I have to ask him?
It's not like I had any reason to believe that she was telling the truth anyway. These questions ran endlessly through my head as tears began to fill my eyes, but his sorry followed soon after and he promised it would never happen again, I went with this and assumed it was because I really did make him angry and we all get angry from time to time.

He seemed to get this kind of angry more often a few weeks after, coming in drunk throwing deadly punches into the back of my neck disabling me from moving fast enough, screaming abuse and accusations. He would leave the next day, locking me inside for hours on end. My hands would be red, sore from the endless bleaching I was doing to make sure everywhere was clean enough and up to his standards, the fear of him coming in and it not being clean, dinner not being cooked and a bath not ran was overpowering. I began calling my mum and deleting all evidence I had done when I knew he was gone just to hear her voice, a part of me desperately wanted to tell her what was happening but the relationship had forced us far apart. We spoke briefly but it was enough to see me through another day, I was never sure when I would see her again because he would never let me leave if we had fought that day, the bruises had to be gone and I had to be fooled enough to come back again.

Some weeks I couldn't leave at all, the shop was directly across the road from his flat and even that posed a risk of me looking at another man. On one occasion we went into his local town centre to purchase meat, the shopkeeper was an elderly man and joked with me about not smiling. Respectfully I smiled and laughed, as soon as we had left the shop apparently that was considered as flirting and I was a filthy whore. This annoyed him till we got home; he grabbed me by my neck as we entered the flat. Just glaring into my eyes, pushing me backwards over a washing machine in the entrance. I fell backwards hurting my back, begging and pleading with him to see how much it was hurting, he told me to be quiet and start cooking. I followed the orders. Whenever he wasn't around I spent hours crying, it was as though I knew this situation was wrong but I couldn't see I had the power to end it by leaving.

> He knew when he needed to be apologetic and act loving and sweet for a couple of days so I would think it was just a phase of me doing something wrong, he had me exactly where he wanted me. I always looked forward to going out in public because a little part of me knew he would be nice even if it was just for 20 minutes while he ate, it was better than nothing. Sometimes people would look at me as though they knew, some women would see the bruises on

my back and look pitiful as I walked by them, it was strange because he was so adamant nobody would believe me yet there were strangers in the world looking at me like they had all the answers. At times now I wish I had listened but I know I would not have learned what I did if I had.

The abuse got worse as time went on, some days he would kick and punch me in my back repeatedly and tell me that a man will never want to love me again and after miscarrying his baby things went from worse to terrible. Just 24 hours after the miscarriage he placed his hand over my mouth, opened my legs and forced himself inside of me. I tried to kick him off and shook my head in fear as he whispered, '' this is for the best''.

I remember the blood and the terrible pain ripping through my stomach and my chest, his hand strangling my mouth caused me to choke on my tears, he threw himself over my body and let out a great sigh. I lay there still, I can't remember much just him turning the shower on and saying to get washed because I was a mess. There was no space for me to be allowed to grieve the miscarriage either and it made things much worse, I don't think anyone can explain the feeling of losing a baby and because I was coming into my third month of pregnancy it made it much more painful and traumatic for me. The whole experience still haunts me to this very day, I still cry when it comes to mothers-day and feel a great sadness in my life because I wasn't given the time when I needed to, to be able to accept it had happened, instead he took it upon himself to blame me in the worst ways possible for things I was not guilty for. I had my physical and human rights taken away by him then he insisted on taking my right to say no to sex away from me too. You become an empty shell just existing in hope that things will change and it is never easy to just leave even when you no longer love the person they hold an obligation over you, one that locks you in for hours on end and removes everyone from your life who would be able to help you. Your resources start running very thin and as much as you want to be free it feels as though there is no way out, people say that women and men who don't leave bring it upon themselves but until you have been in that kind of relationship it can be very hard to understand that it isn't that easy.

We all have trials and tribulations, bad things happen to us, events in our life's that can change how we live forever but we are never alone when we feel like life doesn't treat us fairly or how we feel we deserve to be treated. Sometimes life has already done all it can do to help you see things for what they are and you choose not to listen so life tends to get harder and harder until you do. That's not your fault but it is usually why things can go from bad to worse.

If you are given the signs of an abusive partner, just leave. Don't give them the chance to try and worm their way out of it and end up being exactly what you thought in the first place just know that the signs and the red flags are not in your imagination, they are tried and tested.

If you feel something isn't quite right or something bad may happen if you do a certain thing or go to a certain place, then just do not do it. That feeling you get from your intuition is the most accurate and reliable source of self so listen and act on it. When things happen and they seem unexpected ask yourself if you have had any signals leading up to it, was there something not quite right or was you doing something you shouldn't have been?

I bet you will be able to find an answer that leads to the current situation you find yourself in and it makes getting through it much easier. When we accept that life just needs us to learn in order for us to grow we know that as much as it hurts, we will become much better people because of it and we will be able to help others who experience the same or similar in their life journey.

The relationship came to an end four months later after I had walked in on him on talking to another woman, there was evidence pointing to him cheating like missing condoms and random make up but I was hoping that meant he would leave me.

The relationships end followed one last beating on Easter Sunday 2014. He had jumped from his seat shadowing over me as he pulled me up from my seat and threw me across the room in rage that I dared to argue with him or even speak my feelings over his cheating. I had a new found strength, a voice was telling me that it is fight or flight now and I must fight back. As he held me by my throat over the back of the sofa I began to pull on his jumper and in return he let me go before he mounted his foot onto my pelvic area with a great kick. Falling to the floor I started to look for items in a daze that I could use to knock him out of consciousness so that I could escape.

Throughout this my mum had called my phone and managed to convince him to let me go, pacing up and down he began shouting at me to leave, searching for my phone I staggered out. The pain radiated through my whole body, I began to walk while on the phone to my mum, I turned a corner and was welcomed by a man in his mid-50's. He came over to me and asked what had happened, I couldn't find the words. Carrying me under his arms to keep my balance he took me over to a nearby bench where three girls walking on the street rushed over, I soon found myself in the hospital with doctors looking at my bruised private parts, police in and out, my family flocking in. When I really try to I can even remember the number on the police officers badge, they were talking as if they knew he has this abusive past and that it wasn't anything new. My stomach turned at the thought of him having killed me that night.

The abuse in the relationship was the biggest trial I had ever faced and I felt as though I had been sentenced to life within it and when I was free, even not being with him he still had a hold over me, he was texting me the day after to call him as though nothing had happened and for months I felt scared to leave the house. Being away from him didn't make a difference at all, I still had nightmares of the things he done, my paranoia of him finally getting to me and killing me was so bad that the only way I could sleep properly was if I could sneak myself one to many painkillers. I didn't recognise how badly it had affected me because nobody around me ever wanted to talk about it and soon people stopped asking how I was feeling so I just felt invisible most of the time, disappearing into nothing. The time frame lasted roughly a year and a few months, even when I had started getting emotionally and financially back on track I didn't have any recognition of self, I didn't think I was beautiful or smart because he had told me so many times that I wasn't and my fear of him getting to me was greater than my need to be happy again and that is life destroying.

I found it extremely hard recovering from the abuse and I had experienced a great depression that made me loose hope and self-belief; very quickly I lost weight and was at my smallest size. Most days I considered suicide just to end the nightmares that was made worse by the fact I found it extremely difficult to speak to people about the depth of events within the relationship. As soon as the day began I would start thinking about how to end it, if I wasn't drinking alcohol straight I was crying endlessly for hours.

None of it made any sense so I couldn't grasp a better understanding, I found that family and friends soon lost interest and this angered me. It was a very lonely time for me and I only ever had the comfort of my mum, it was enough but at the same time it wasn't, you find a greater dependency for peoples love and comfort when you have lost sense of love and comfort for yourself.

When we consider abusive partners it is extremely important that we know what red flags signal towards the situation being a bad one. Here are some important things to look out for:

1. Unreasonable jealousy
   It is okay for a partner to think you are the most amazing person and that everyone should know that you are with him or her but not within unreasonable measures. A relationship does not mean that you are someone's property, if you notice that your partner feels this way about you and causes arguments concerning the people you are around or the things you do; I will advise that this is only going to get worse and should be taken as a very serious warning sign.

2. Possessiveness
   All of a sudden your partner must look through your phone, must know your whereabouts and who, what, where and why you are wanting to go there, or why your friend dare to text you. Maybe him or her says it is because they want to protect you but this is not the case, they just want full control of everything that you do.

3. Constant put-downs
   The compliments have stopped now and you are fat or ugly, dumb or stupid every other day and if you dare to wear anything they have not approved it is disgusting and you

need to sort it out. Well you are not any of those things and anyone who loves you will never say them to you, stop thinking it is a joke or light-hearted. It is the start of many more emotionally verbal destructive forms of abuse.

### 4. Guilt Trips

Everything is now your fault! He forgot milk because well you are alive and breathing. Everything that does not go to his favour is because of you even the thing that you have no involvement in. The arguments are your fault and be aware that when they start to physically abuse you, this will all be your fault too.

### 5. Saying '' I love you but.''

There should never be but condition to how your partner loves you, love is love and when someone does love you they will not look for reasons to make you ever feel like they don't. Abusers want you to think they love you but with conditions that you then feel like you have to change so they love you properly but it is just because they do not love you at all.

### 6. Control

You no longer have a say in anything that happens, they pick the dinner and you cook it. I bet you don't even have a say in your clothes, your hair or when you can and can't talk. People were not made to be controlled in relationships, your partner is supposed to embrace you and the things that you want to do. If this is currently or is becoming a problem, it will not get any better.

It is very important you remember that it is not your fault. Abusers are experts at manipulating us into believing that the way they act is due to something we have done. They are aware of your insecurities and they use them against you. Abusers have the ability to convince you that you do not deserve any better and that they treat you this way because they are helping you to become better. Most abusers act very charming around people so they don't suspect what happens, this can be very confusing. Know that if you recognise these signs there is little hope for this relationship to ever get any better, it would take too much for the abuser to change. I urge you to leave and seek them the help they desperately need before it spirals out of control with another partner. I know you may love this person but they do not love or respect you. I promise that you will get over them sooner if you break it off earlier than if you experience what will come, on the guarantee that you would ever even survive.

>The nightmares still haunt me often, I get upset and cry over the situation and wish I had listened to people. There are friendships I was never able to fix but I understand their reasoning and despite that they were a great support system after the relationship. A majority of it was due to the fact I became very shut off from people, I didn't understand what it was I needed to do with myself to feel even remotely normal again, if there is such a thing. When I do feel myself slipping into feeling sad about it I remind myself that I still survived it regardless of the hurt and the loss I had felt throughout, I made it through and I am so proud of myself for that.

Toxic;

*" Poisonous substances which can live inside of people who claim to love us"*

The greatest risk we pose to ourselves is our un-ability to notice when we are keeping ourselves in toxic situations with friends, jobs or partners. Naturally we do ignore the signs and then expose ourselves to issues with depression, stress and anxiety. If life unexpectedly takes us on a path we did not intend for ourselves, we will automatically assume we are failing and falling into these emotional states of mind that breed depression. I have seen many young girls say they have failed because college didn't work out, their job does not make them happy and they feel like they have not achieved what they want to. This does not make you a failure it just makes your purpose incomplete, the situation you are in is because of a choice you have made and the only way out is based on the choices that you make next.

Failure is never your final destination unless you let it be, anything that is not serving you or making you happy can be changed even if it takes a long time or is hard work. The change is what you desire to feel achieved so the effort is what you must make; understandably this can be made difficult when we are also around toxic people. We don't always even recognise how destructive this is, people naturally tend to seek advice and guidance from the people in their lives whether this is family or friends it may not always be the advice that you need. Not everyone around us has our best interests at heart and not everyone really wants us to be better than them and sometimes the only way for them to stop this from happening is to invade your thoughts with negativity. If someone you consider as a close friend is telling you not to pursue a job or act on a passion because you lack in something you will most likely listen because you trust his or her judgement in your life. What you are unable to see is just how much you can achieve those things and how much that scares them, this isn't to say all friends feel or act this way but you must remain aware to the ones that do. True friends and real lovers won't find pleasure in embracing your flaws and any dreams you do have they will naturally want to encourage you to complete and vice versa.

If you are reading this and feel like you may be a toxic friend or presence in somebody's life intentionally or unintentionally I want you to know that this doesn't necessarily make you a bad person it just signals that something is drastically missing in your own life, it could be something you are aware of or something you need to discover but whatever it may be it is stopping you applauding others so it needs to be resolved. Maybe you are un-happy about something you have experienced or you are finding it difficult to work on your purpose and seek ambition within your life choices. If this is the case, I suggest you take some time to soul search and leave people alone until you feel happier with yourself because nobody deserves the backlash of your current misery. Some people really need someone to tell them it is going to be okay and that they can achieve their dreams so I am telling you exactly that.

Your friends or partner will prefer you much more if you respectably take the time to go and discover more about you first so you are less concerned with keeping people at the same level of unhappiness or incompletion you currently feel.

Being able to recognize that you may be toxic is the first step to removing those bad and selfish thoughts from your mind so don't feel bad on yourself for knowing that you are this way just be willing to change. With being toxic comes greater unhappiness when you notice that friends, family and employers do not like you. There will be times in life that you are unable to meet your potential because people can recognise how toxic you are so they do their best to avoid you and it won't help how you feel. Learn to accept whatever has caused this mind-set, accept an apology you probably have no received and rid you of it. Tell yourself that it is no longer holding your life hostage, speak this daily until you speak it without having to tell yourself too, this is a good sign that your subconscious is aware of it now and wants you to continue life believing it. It is never easy coming to the realisation that you may not have been a very nice person and people around you are badly affected by your ways but it is much better to realise and solve it than to carry on.

Sometimes life can be going so well then all of a sudden we are stuck in time with the weight of the world on our backs. It always seems much easier to crack and fall to the floor then it is to keep going, carrying the weight and holding onto hope but by giving in we don't give ourselves the chance to learn about what it is to win in victory over life's unfortunate events. That is all they are, events that are unfortunate and unfortunately so given to us, they are not the final destination that we will ever find ourselves in and they certainly won't be the only ones that we ever have to face in life so if we only ever give up how will we ever truly experience what it is to keep going. Everything needs a pinch of bad to balance out the good it is just how we choose to deal with it which makes all the difference, there are events that are particularly more difficult than others such as grief and loosing someone which can have very detrimental especially if they played a big role in our way of life. Adjusting to how we feel about life after loss can be very depressive and life changing but how we choose to accept death as we do life is always our choice, remember that death is the only thing we can be sure will happen in life so we have to learn to grieve for a period of time then go through the process of acceptance. Learning to accept things in life always makes dealing with them much easier, the same rule applies to self-acceptance. When we learn to accept ourselves, our flaws and the things that make us different, we learn to deal with them in a much better way.

After suffering two miscarriages I learned a lot about my strength and even when I really wanted to give up somewhere, something gave me the power to get up and keep going. I don't think I can even explain it or understand it but it happened each and every time I told myself that I could no longer carry on. It was never my time to give up and give in, there was hope for me always to do more and be more even if I didn't believe at that specific time that it could ever be possible. Life has a way of testing our ability to see past the bad and keep going and even when it may not feel like it life is rooting for you to keep going. We aren't destined to be given bad and not get out of it, life wants us to go through it and learn how to get back out of it for more reasons than one. Very often it has much to do with life trying to help us find our purpose through the painful lessons because we didn't pay much attention to the ones prior to that which probably didn't cause as much pain so didn't seem so important.

Self- acceptance;

*" Being able to accept everything about you without requiring the validation of another person"*

When the trials and tribulations that we go through begin to have an adverse effect on our feelings about self we have to focus back on self-acceptance and remember that how we feel about ourselves is the starting point for many things in our life. Self-acceptance always begins with recognising what it is that flags as a problem, whether it be something we are unhappy with or what other people tend to highlight, we have to be able to accept them as a part of us and move on from the negatives about it. The negative doesn't and never will make it feel any better, if you focus so long on the bad how can you ever see and feel what is good about it, finding positives doesn't always have to be such a hard task.

What it is that you struggle to accept, write it down on a piece of paper and pin point the things about it that are not bad. For example, if it is that you have put weight on you can say a positive is that you can still lose weight. If it is that you don't like the way you look a positive is that there is nobody else in the world who will look as good as you do in your skin so you should feel proud of who you are regardless.  There is always a positive in every bad thing we just have to look hard enough, finding them brings us even closer to resolving them because everything stops feeling so impossible. The longer we look at the cant's the longer we won't be able to find the resolution for it

Dear Depression

For those who are currently going through depression I would like to tell you how amazing you are, I know how difficult it is, how painful it is to be stuck in absolute darkness with no insight into finding the light but I also want you to know that the light is not far away. Depression is not to be taken lightly and if you are feeling extreme bouts of sadness and suicidal thoughts I urge you to please seek medical help, during my experiences medication did not help me but it may be different for you, sometimes you might just need someone to talk to and a safe evaluation of your state of mind because no matter how you feel you are so deserving of life.

There is something sinister about asking life for the best and always finding yourself hurt or at a loss, it isn't as though we have done something to life to deserve feeling such deep and unexplainable pain.

The depression for me was a very deep abys, like a sinking feeling which left my whole body feeling numb, from the top of my head to the tip of my toes it felt like nothing could change how deeply sad I was.

Many things can lead to feeling depressed and sometimes the trigger is well hidden, usually because it is something we don't want to face or accept in our lives and that is understandable, at times it may be something from our childhood that has found its way back into our lives and is haunting us. The trigger whatever it may be can be resolved and there are many ways to do this but first and foremost we have to try and work out exactly what it is, no matter how hard it may be to do this.

A good way to begin this is to start your own logbook where you document all your negative thoughts and feelings, evaluate them and ask yourself are they really worth the space they are consuming?
Can they be changed?
Are you even to blame?

If you can't change them and they are not your fault then just let them go, do not allow them to define who you are and the happiness that you feel. Feeling down is natural but feeling unworthy of life or taking guilt for things that you have not done is not and you deserve to feel as fantastic as you are.

If there is something that makes you feel even slightly better like music for example, use this and to your advantage so that whenever the sad feeling kicks in you have something to distract you from focusing on it. Also make sure that the people you are around are positive and not judgemental towards the feelings that you have. Most positive people will be happy to reveal the things that help them to maintain a happier state of mind so learn from them.

Keep in mind that misery loves company and it can be hard to stay away from negative people who feel like you do but do your best to avoid them. Neither of you are helping each other by confirming one another's fears. Feeling down breeds on its own feelings and you start to convince yourself that you don't deserve to enjoy anything, the resolve for this is to do things that you used to enjoy, one fun thing a day to keep the depression away is my saying.

When I found myself in depression it was being around the right people that helped me to forget for a while how deeply sad I was and when suicidal thoughts did arise I thought of those same people, my mum, nieces and siblings. I imagined how deeply sad they would be without me and knew that even if I didn't know my purpose yet I had a purpose within their lives and their hearts, I didn't want to make them grieve for me no matter how sad I felt inside. Unfortunately, some people don't have anyone to view like this and I know it will be harder to understand but you should know that you and everyone else living and breathing on the earth has a purpose to me and each other, someone somewhere will need to hear about how you survived. I may need to hear how you survived one day too, you may just be the person to save someone else's life, and we all hold the possibility so no matter how we feel we all have a purpose to be alive for.

> Another thing I found very useful was watching motivational videos and speeches, it really played a big difference in how I viewed my life and myself too; I began to learn about depression and what I could still achieve. Seeing how other people who had suffered and how others suffering more have overcome their challenges inspired me to do the exact same thing and find my happy.

> Don't live your life feeling bad for making decisions that make you happy in concern to your own life, if these things accept people it is not an issue for you to take on because you are not responsible for their happiness if they cannot be happy for you. People who want you to live in misery for their happiness should not be allowed a space in your life. You should ensure that the people around you want you to begin making choices that will result in you being happy this includes family and friends. You are responsible for your happy so if you can find something that provides this

don't allow people to stand in the way of it, maybe it means someone else gets less of your time and hears less of how sad you are but this shouldn't matter if it means that when they do hear from you they will hear of much happier you are. Everyone in your life should only want what is best for you and your happiness regardless of it makes them feel otherwise because your job before anything is to make sure that you are happy. Of course you must be a good person but when it concerns you being happy at times we have to be selfish and put that before anyone and anything.

There are many different types of depression, which is why you must seek medical help; it is a good idea to look into your family history to just to see if any relatives have suffered with depression because this can cause genetic links. Be prepared to be honest and open about events in your life leading up to these feelings with your doctor so they can evaluate the best form of help and reasoning for your benefit, if you are not completely honest you will prolong the time in which you can get the help needed.

Some day's depression made me feel so full of life that I could have burst and others so dead that I didn't even know if my heart was still beating or not, it was a dark and very miserable house to live in when depression was the foundation. No matter how many times I tried to move out I found myself being dragged right back in again and it was starting to feel like I would be stuck at that address for the rest of my life, I had packed my bags more than once but it didn't make a difference because when depression locked the door I could never find the key. It is a very hard place to be in and people don't always understand this and you have to accept that it is okay if they don't, all that matters is your wellbeing and you finding a path to recovery. It is so vital that you know you are never alone, many people suffer with depressive outbursts but never speak out sometimes out of fear and others because they assume it will just go away but it don't. Depression needs you but you do not need depression always keep that in mind, it needs you to sleep all day and cry all night because if you don't, depression will lose control of the hold it has over you. It is about being able to fight the urges of complete sadness and despair, saying,

'' Today I will not spend the day in bed, I will drag myself out and I will do something that will make me feel better''.

Spend five minutes of your day writing down things that you feel grateful for, it can be as simple as ''my parents love me'' or ''fresh coffee''.

Whatever it is that you feel grateful for take the time to remind yourself of those things to keep you in good spirit.

When you do start to go against depression you will find that depression puts up a very big fight just to test you and prove a point but you don't have to let it win, ever. You can take your power back just by believing that you can in the first place. Depression doesn't like you to believe that you could actually be happy again so let depression know that you will be, start speaking it out loud, tell yourself every day that you WILL be happy again and you WILL be okay.

Notice how even on the bad days those simple words will make a difference, I promise that no matter how bad it gets it can get better, you can dig yourself out of that deep, dark hole.

I believe in you.

You-niverse

*'' Your unique, beautiful and special energy space in which you deposit your thoughts ''*

Karma, Mantra & Taking Control

I had spent many years of my life thinking that everything bad in my life was due to the fact I had no control or say in what happens, assuming that it was happening because I was just unlucky. I wasn't aware of how much control I really had over everything that happens to me just like you do too. Bad will happen because it is always needed to balance with the abundance of good you can determine that you receive, it is an easy process which just requires us to really want to see changes.

The universe became my you-niverse and I realised that everything in my life at that current time was down to everything I needed to become and everything·I was thinking. We do need some of the bad we have experienced if not just to teach us a lesson but to also expand our minds for a better understanding of ourselves and how we think and act. Universal laws do apply to everything that we do and karma is the most important one you should become familiar with. Karma states that for every action there will be a reaction and a person cannot escape the consequences, we are held accountable for our thoughts and our actions. It is the intention behind our thoughts and actions that trigger the cause and effect reaction of our you-niverse. It is like saying if we want happiness, peace, love and good friendships then we should BE happy, loving, peaceful and a good friend. This is because what we are ejecting into the universe, the universe will place back into our you-niverse.

> As we are on our journey through this life we will meet people who our souls recognise so you may be assuming that you meet the people you mean to meet and this is great if the people you do meet in this life have a mind like yours and can offer you support but if these people provide the opposite they will become a negative aspect in our life. For example, women alike me who continued to get with physically and mentally abusive men did so because that is what he had known, and until we become aware of self, who we are, where we are and what our purpose is in the now, we continued to repeat that cycle. This is cause and effect, if you allow karma the ability to work with both your subconscious and conscious thoughts turning into actions you will find that you stop bringing suffering and bad luck into your own life.
>
> You have to view karma as your own reality-mirror to see the inner you. The human karmic wave means that every seven years our circumstances will change in reflection of our actions from the seven years previous. This means that if you have spent the past seven years being a kind, loving and peaceful person the next seven years will reflect that and you will receive in abundance happiness, peace and love.

What you are seeing today is a product of how you acted seven years ago. Anything negative that you are inflicting into the universe will come back to you seven years later. A negative, destructive life will be rewarded seven years later with a negative, destructive reality. It may seem easier to be destructive to others but it won't be as fun when it is returned to you, understanding that what we do today can come back to us several years later can be a great motivation towards adopting a more positive reality. A healthy attitude and thought process towards yourself generates health for you over the next seven-year period, karma can be positive and can help you to dig out negative attitudes.

We also fail to realise how powerful our thoughts are when it concerns progressing towards our goals in life, very often we are subconsciously playing a voice that is telling us we are not enough. If we are not conscious of this happening, we believe it to be true. Our actions have to always align with our thoughts so if we are thinking these negative things they are exactly what we become.

A good tool of progression is getting hold of our subconscious thoughts and using NDT, negative distraction tools to allow the right flow of thoughts into our conscious.
A good NDT is the use of your whys.

Why are you trying to think well?
Why are you trying to improve your life?

Maybe it is that you have children and want to create the best life for them or you are currently tired of how life is for you and want to elevate into more happiness. Whatever your why is, use it. Speak it to yourself and repeat it.

Getting in tune with your you-niverse will require the right amount of '' I CAN ''. Use your why like you would use a mantra; repeat it as many times throughout the day as you need to for it to become a part of your reality. If anyone attempts to doubt your journey use your whys to show him or her how wrong, they are.

This is just one NDT; another is creating a dream board. This is a really good tool for people who are creative and learn with visualisation because you can actually see everything that you want to achieve. This tool means that you place your subconscious at this better place, and then telling your conscious it is yours. You just don't have access to it yet. People may confuse this NDT with trickery of the mind but is actually a powerful tool that people use to attract the things that they want in life, similar to the law of attraction but using imagery that we become familiar with. Using pictures of the things you want: cars, house, job, lifestyle and family. Stick them onto a canvas or create this on your phone, add a timescale for when you want to achieve them. Have this somewhere you can see it every day, begin to manifest in the idea that you are there with these things and they are yours because you are enough to make it happen.

> You will begin to notice that your subconscious has a desire to accessing these things without you having to control it. It is never about other people so nobody need feel as though you are showing more than you have, it is about self and allowing your manifestation into the correct energies for the outcomes that you want out of life.
>
> You can also create your own mantra's, which will aid your concentration and focus on getting to where you want to be and achieving what you want to achieve. My personal mantra is,

'' I am the master of my results. I am the driving force towards all I do''.

Using mantras are a good way of keeping your mind full of purposeful energy. When creating your own essential elements to consider is creating a phrase that you know you are actually going to confidently state and apply to your day in a positive way. You must focus it on the things you want not the things you want to avoid, stating your desires by only using positive words avoiding 'can't'. You can't just say it either you have to feel what you are repeating at a heightened state of feeling gratitude, strength, appreciation, love and pride about what you are repeating, feeling and knowing as if you already have it.

Naturally it will take time and patience for you to get familiar with your mantra but being consistent will help.
Repeat it every day as many times throughout the day. Saying it without thinking about saying it will install it into your subconscious. This form of attraction and NDT will also give you the power of positive to stand against failures in life. I had started finding it much easier to blame everyone else for my bad luck and misfortunes, it was my parents fault for not being together or my ex partners fault for cheating on me because it was much harder to say that I had choices and I made bad ones. The blame game eventually wore thin and nothing ever changed. I found that by not taking responsibility I was never able to make it better.

Taking responsibility should never be confused with self-blame. It is being able to see how you can get desired outcomes in life by knowing how to correct yourself along the way. If you are not where you hoped to be five years ago take responsibility for this and ask yourself what you need to do, what you haven't done and how you can change it. When you do realise that everything you ever are and everything you will ever become is down to you and the choices you make, you will be able to get rid of the negative excuse making, that can prevent you from succeeding in life. It can seem like an awfully big responsibility but when we have come to that realisation we are also able to see that we can achieve and accomplish anything that we want to and anything that we believe we can do; we can get done. The acknowledgment for our responsibilities in life makes achieving things much easier because it erases the negativity that comes from always blaming other people, life or bad events for why you don't seem to be currently succeeding.

One of our biggest issues can be that we do not like to fail, it doesn't feel good or make you feel like things are possible for you and more importantly so we don't like people to see us fail, however when you start accepting the failure as your responsibility you will also find a solution to avoiding failure again.

Learn to forgive people for the mistakes that they make, mistakes are inevitable we all make them and we more often so don't mean to make them in the first place, learning to forgive yourself for the mistakes you make and the mistakes of others will help make it seem easier to accept them. If you mess up there is no point in beating yourself up over it no matter how big or how small, the time you spend investing negative and hateful feelings towards yourself for messing up is time you could spend accepting it and learning from it. The same applies to when other people mess up too, don't hold it against them. Clinging onto a desire to blame them will shift the focus away from your need to take responsibility of you and your own life.

If you feel burdened by the people in your life by anyway it is best that you let those people go, it isn't your responsibility to take care of your friends lives or success it is theirs and yours is for you. That doesn't mean that you shouldn't be kind to people or offer them a helping hand it means that you are not obligated to anyone's downfalls or mistakes in life when they are not your fault and when they are it is entirely your responsibility to be sorry for and learn from.

We are born with an obligation to ourselves, when we choose to become parents we obligate ourselves to their lives until they are adults and should teach them the same thing. When we see people who have been raised by parents who do not take responsibility they end up duplicating that behaviour and never feeling like anything bad they do is their own fault. If we teach children that yes, if you throw your juice on the floor it is your fault, they will learn to stop doing it and carry a sense of responsibility for self into their adult lives.

Your Purpose

Failure in life is never the end all and be all, it is a pause in time to allow you to re-consider your approach and how you are currently choosing to deal with things in life, it gives you the opportunity to assess everything and find a new way of dealing with it. If your business doesn't work out it is because, how you are choosing to start it is not the correct way for you it doesn't mean that it will never work. The most important way to view failure is to take it as a big learning curve that is sent to help you grow, if you never fail in your life you will never really learn how to succeed. It is part of a process that requires you to pay close attention and take note of the things that caused it so you don't repeat the mistakes again, it seems easier to take failure as life telling you no but it is important that you view it as life just saying try again.

When it concerns trying to achieve goals a big concept is your state of mind and how you approach what it is that you are trying to achieve, creating a W-E-A-L-T-H mind-set is a good way to begin.

W- Write down what you want
E- Envision your future
A – Affirm your desires
L- Listen to your inner voice
T- Take action & transform
H- Hold the vision

Training your mind to work with you to achieve your maximum potential is very important and will make the difference between achieving your goals and slowly working towards them. If your mind is in a state that encourages your achievability then you will find yourself on the right path, everything you think you can do is everything that you will end up getting done.

See yourself in your dream job, driving your dream car and going home to your dream house.

Wake up every day and see that vision in your mind then start to tell yourself it is yours you just can't access it yet. Repeat it every day and set the affirmation into your subconscious mind so you don't even have to think about saying it, you just do. Treat every new day as a stepping stone towards making these mental images a reality, wear your success in the form of a smile every day, dress well and feel the confidence leak through into your energy. People magnetize to confident people, notice how many more people want to know your goals and desires in life and how many of them will take you seriously when you choose to manifest in the right vibrations.

When something doesn't feel right, don't do it and when something feels like it has something to offer, give it a go don't fear stepping out of your comfort zone because it is the areas surrounding it which offers the most amount of growth and prosperity. Choosing to stay in one place your whole life will never allow you to grow anywhere but where you already are, it's a never ending cycle like walking round and round in a circle unable to find the exit when all along it was the entrance. It never makes sense yet it is always so simple, enabling yourself the life away from what feels comfortable will really open up doors for you.

Everyone likes the feeling of comfort and for some people what offers comfort stays as their safe place and anything besides that would be far too dangerous to step into, it becomes a pattern of life that we can find very hard to break out of. We get so used to repeating our daily tasks that we get scared to ever do anything other than that when it is most likely something completely different which will place us closer to what we want out of life. Some people even assume that they don't know what it is they want yet because they haven't given themselves the time and space to grow out and away from anything or anyone who keeps them in one place. Being able to set yourself free and see all the option doors available to you will help you to establish exactly what it is that you want out of your life and what your purpose is.

Finding your purpose doesn't always have to seem like such a big scary task when you actually feel ready, it is about removing yourself from everything current, evaluating it and finding your happy place. Your purpose will never make you sad or miserable, it isn't a job or relationship that should make you feel bad or unexcited. Your purpose should wake you up every day before the alarm clock has even gone off.

Let's say growing up you love to dance so you think that when you finish school you will work towards being a dance teacher or a professional dancer but at some point dancing stops being something you love and you feel stuck because you have no idea what else you are good at so you feel like a failure that doesn't know what he or she wants. Wrong.

You are a person who has grown away from something that was only temporary, this applies to hobbies, jobs, friendships and relationships. Life has a way of moving us on from anything that is just '' a moment in time'' something that fills the now but won't make us feel good forever and it is something we should be thankful for because if life never shifted us from it we would live a very miserable life. The problem is that sometimes we think it means we have no place on the earth now because we invested our all into something that we no longer see purpose in when in fact it means that we now have time to learn something new about ourselves, find something that fulfils us permanently and makes us feel good from the inside out. We can feel sad for the temporary pleasures but we shouldn't dwell on them as something that is destructive to our purpose it is something that is actually helping us move closer to finding exactly what it is.

Some people have the tendency to flicker from hobby to a new job to a new friend very easily and usually so the problem is a lot deeper than what floats on the surface, they may have issues with self or a problem arising from abandonment and these people require the most amount of reassurance that they will settle. If you find that you get bored of jobs quickly or you have a problem with staying in a long term relationship, try to assess what it is that makes you feel as though you can no longer stay in that particular thing.

Learn what it is that stops you from settling and avoid that. It isn't healthy to be uncommitted to things in life and it can be a pattern that sticks with people for the whole of their lives for them to get to an elder age and wish they had stuck at one thing, take the time to truly get to know yourself and what it is that really makes you feel a good that you haven't felt before.

For many of us there is a gap between the life we are leading and the people that we feel we really are. Too many of us spend large portions of our lives doing jobs that we may not believe in or feel truly motivated by. This is a big missed opportunity and a major source of stress.

We all have strengths and talents, but we don't often recognize them and use them day to day.

Write down a list of 5 to 8 things that you're really good at. Things that just come naturally to you. We all have things that we're passionate about and love to do too, but very often we think of these things as hobbies rather than involving them at the heart of our life and work.

Then write down a list of 5 to 8 things that you're passionate about. Things you love to experience, talk about, think about and do.

Breaking your purpose down into categories is a good way to start, find the subject matter in regards to it being a job, being a parent, being a husband or wife maybe something as adventurous as living in a different country so you can make a change somewhere else, if you can vision yourself doing it and feeling good doing it every day then that is a good step forward. Researching what you will have to do to make it possible is the next thing, do you need qualifications? Is your partner ready for children or do you have to take alternative routes? How much will it cost and where can you get support?

Having a solid understanding will make it much easier to achieve because no un-expected surprises can pop up along the way and catch you off guard, you should be fully prepared and ready.

Always remember that your purpose will be unique and individual to you, don't worry about what other people spend their time doing or why they do it, focus your time and energy into doing what you need to do to create a positive and purposeful life for yourself. Nobody else will be able to give you what you want out of life, no matter how kind or caring they may come across as, your purpose is for you to develop and master.

## Stop creating a life based on people's opinions.

The fastest way to create a life you do not enjoy is to base it on what other people say and feel about you, if all you do is live to please them when do you make time to please yourself?

We have briefly touched on self-love but I urge you to understand how important this is, not only does it stop you from being emotionally reliant upon people it also develops your confidence, self- esteem, self-worth and speeds up the process to creating a life you love. It is near impossible for you to enjoy your life while you are basing it entirely on what other people say, this can include things as small as what you wear. When you start choosing to dress for their validation you give them control over an area in your life and this will end up spiralling out of control, before you know it you will find yourself living on their every demand.

Seeking validation leads to you giving up a right to your own life and placing it into the hands of strangers, why would they want to take your life and make it good when that would dim the shine on their life?

It is human nature to be self-conscious and have insecurities, but you cannot allow them to dictate the person you are or what you are able to do. View them as challenges to better yourself, place them in your life as stepping stones not problems that need other people's opinions to improve. I once heard a woman say that how many likes' you get on social media can determine how liked you are in real life; it is a frightening cycle that leads you into the middle of nowhere. If you really believe that likes can equal to what is important in life, you will never stop living for them. The best thing for you to do is make sure that the friendships you allow into your life are genuine and not forced, don't ever try to change yourself just to fit into a certain group. Let your true colours show, the people who will love the real you are the people with whom you should be friends with.

Life is too short to live it trying to please everyone.

[ You are beautiful, amazing, smart and funny with or without their say so, you are a diamond who shines without other people's sunlight

*Dear Broken Woman*
*You are so delicate and special, out of the many women in the world you had to be broken. It has to feel like there is no glue strong enough to put you back together, you have to feel at the end of the road. This isn't because you deserve it, this is because you have the ability to overcome more than you know right now.*

*I bet you wake up every morning after nights of crying, paint on a smile and face the world. You probably have more prospects then some women with no problems in the world at all, your issues don't make you any less of a success story or a beautiful woman they just place you on the map where there is growth and prosperity. The pain you have been feeling is not permanent, it is a moment in time that has been sent to show you the world in a new light.*

*Yes, you are allowed to refuse people entry into your life, don't feel bad for avoiding people who do not know that right now you need to be treated with love and care. Take your time to heal, avoid jumping from man to man, I promise you they won't ever be able to heal what is broken, that is your job. Once you are able to find all the pieces of the puzzle, the right man will never bring you back to this horrible, destructive place again.*

The Cheating Man

If you have found yourself here I figure you want to know why you have been cheated on by a man or maybe just maybe you are the cheating man, I won't sugar coat reality and tell you that it's okay, there is no good in cheating or being cheated on and more often than none the man cheats because he can. I can break down several reasons but none will be as straightforward and honest as the fact that it is simply because he can and he probably thinks he won't get caught and even when he does he will still try to lie his way out of it, because he can. Sometimes it is because we allow ourselves to allow it to happen, we accept the first time as a mistake then we complain when it happens again, and again.

Cheaters don't wake up one day and decide that they don't want to do it again, temptation is temptation and if they can't fight it yesterday they won't fight it tomorrow. A lot of it has to do with the fact the cake seems much tastier to the cheating man when he can have more than one slice, you could be the most attractive, smartest, goal driven woman with everything going for you, if he wants more cake he will go out and eat it. A man who has not yet learned to be content cannot be raised to know better by a woman who wants him to, her wanting him to is not enough to do the job, it is entirely his responsibility.

When we look into the childhood and pasts of the cheating man many of them grew up in situations that give us red flag signs, of course not every man whose dad cheated on his mum will cheat but there are some who will never learn no better. Some had parents who time and time again shown the cheating man it is okay to cheat and lie. Some mums don't even know their son is watching every time she forgives his dad for having sexual relations with another woman and continues to act as though everything is okay, this isn't to say every man will grow up thinking it is acceptable but we only act on what we absorb as children.

More than likely he will follow the path that was shown to him, as children do. We don't think about these things in our relationships because we usually make the mistake of assuming that we won't ever be ''stupid'' enough to end up in love with the cheating man when little do we know even the ''smartest'' woman ends up in that web at least once in her life.

Sometimes we think ''well we have good sex, he says he's happy and I am so there could never be the chance of him cheating''. Wrong. You could have the best sex he has had in his life, that won't stop him from wanting to try more elsewhere because a lot of cheating men believe that there could always be better, quicker fixes with no strings attached.

With his partner he has to attend family functions, take her on dates, listen to her problems and tend to her needs but with the women he cheats on her with he doesn't have to do anything to get what he wants, it's easier and meaningless to him so he doesn't feel as though he is doing anyone harm. Little does the cheating man know more often than none women have tendencies to get emotionally attached to sex as much as they do flowers and cute dates. They assume that because he is willing to cheat with her or if she doesn't know he is cheating she will figure he is choosing to sleep with her because he ''likes'' her, not every woman has the same standards and for some sex is enough to make up their mind. Once she has decided that he is into her she will scheme on making it official, this is where the cheating man always gets caught, once she finds a way to contact his woman or she discovers he has one believe me she will set out to destroy that, feelings are not something to be played with.

Of course the cheating man does not think she would ever be so heartless and mean because only he can hurt his partner, right?

This new age world we live in doesn't make it any easier for the cheating man or the women, everyone is so accessible via social media and some women have a lot more on offer so it can be extremely hard for eyes to not end up in places they shouldn't be and before you know it numbers to be exchanged. We can't control how society has developed but a good man won't have the interests of social media because he will feel content with the woman he has, if you find that a man is very interested in his Instagram account don't assume it is just for entertainment purposes, you can get women literally throwing their private parts at men on there so if he isn't making it known that he has his woman please don't be surprised when you are not the only one.

It is a choice he is making and as wrong as the woman is, how was she to know he is taken if he decided not to tell her?

We have all heard the saying that men cheat on their beautiful women with less attractive women and some of us may feel we have been a victim of that, we forget that looks is not the only way to determine how a man feels, a woman could be very attractive with morals but not be very confident and for some men that can be draining whereas you could find a less attractive woman with no morals who is full of energy and excitement, it can be intoxicating being around women like that for men. Very often there is something missing within the relationship, it could be something as simple as differing senses of humour or something much bigger like a lack of communication, whatever it may be it can drive weaker men into the arms of another woman. Men like to be with women who make them and their ego feel good so beauty becomes irrelevant, if all he has is something good to look at he will eventually lose interest and seek someone who gives him more than a pretty face.

Beauty is a matter of mind and for some men it is the first factor they think they want before any other, until they land themselves a total babe who is more interested in how she has applied her make-up than how he feels, eventually he will get tired of just having someone attractive on his arms and want someone who tends to his emotional desires. This doesn't apply to every case, all rounded women get cheated on too, through absolute no fault of their own, in those cases it is usually because the man is just a cheater who has no interest in settling down as of yet and she is his unfortunate victim. He may have general feelings for her but not enough to make him remain loyal to her.

It is a destructive cycle that can only be prevented when we refuse to allow ourselves to be treated that way and men you stop allowing yourself to cheat, by all means if you want to live a life that serves you by being with multiple women do it on your own don't be so selfish that you want to do it while you are in a relationship. If as a man you have been cheated on and you find it hard to understand why, you cheating on innocent women will not give you the answers it will make you feel like a bad person when you finally realize the effects of what you have done.

If you have found yourself a victim of the cheating man take my word for it, it is not your fault even if you didn't stimulate him enough it was his choice to let you know and let you go. There is still such thing as love but now isn't the time to rush yourself back into looking for it, take your time to heal and allow your mind to accept that it was not your fault. If you do try to jump into another relationship you will find that you are not trusting, you will be very paranoid and end up hurting someone who may not deserve it.

> Getting over issues with trusting men is never easy but it is a process that can be made possible by avoiding them for a while and staying away from '' empty dating''.

Don't date for fun or to think it will help you get over what has happened it will only make you dislike men even more because there will be no strings and no feelings attached to the situation so nobody will have any loyalties to each other. There is nothing wrong with enjoying some '' you time''.

Get to grips with your self-worth now you know exactly what it is, value the lessons you have learned and allow them to help you move forward for yourself. As hard and emotionally disturbing as it is you will find a route out and the best is to use the time for yourself, learn what it is about yourself that you love and make that the centre of your world, follow through with what makes you feel good about yourself and your life. You have taken your power back now so until you are ready to trust someone with that again it is yours, use it wisely.

*[ definition/ Good Man – A man who respects, honours and provides for his queens emotional and spiritual desires. He offers in abundance, love, loyalty and support of her dreams, working with her to achieve the best life possible]*

<u>Stop saying that all men are bad, give credit where due.</u>

*Not every man should be placed under the '' every man '' category, you probably can't see that the world is made up of good men too because you keep them as friends or dismiss them as to boring. If there were no good men in the world, there would be no such thing as love, we don't love bad people but we do chose to let them into our lives. In some situations, we pick the wrong man over the right one all along and have to spend years learning from this, give credit to the good man you should of pursued, forgive the bad ones, forgive yourself for making a bad choice and don't paint them all with the same brush.*

[ success] – the joy of completing goals you set for yourself.

Using Your Self-Worth Too Attract Success

Having a sense of self-worth is very important, it affects your self-image and defines your level of confidence, which means that if you have a high regard for yourself then you will have more self-confidence and confidence in yourself will help you achieve more things on your own— even those things that you normally are not capable of doing.

Aside from this, it also dictates a large majority of your happiness. A person who is content and satisfied with how his or her life is will be the happiest person in the world and it does not matter what other people think or say about them because they won't believe it. When you have high self-worth, you would not really care about what other people have to say about you, because you are pretty sure about who you are as a person and what you can do. Some people go through their lives without really realizing that they have very low regard for themselves. Many people are too preoccupied with their everyday struggles that they fail to focus on the most important things like overcoming difficulties and feeling good about themselves.

    Ask yourself:
    Do you value yourself?
    Do you have enough respect for yourself?

    People who can answer yes confidently will know that because they do this they have attracted much more positivity and progression in their lives. For those of you thinking you are un-sure the answer is simply no, you should never be in-between feeling good about yourself and respecting yourself, you either do or you don't. Some people, sadly, think too low of themselves. Despite the great things in their lives, they convince themselves otherwise and they wallow in the bad and the frustrating, they have such low regard for themselves that they do not think they deserve anything in life. These people are not dreamers, because they think that dreams are only for children and they understand that they should accept their life as it is, and not want to make more for themselves. They are prone to quitting and they reject opportunities because they are so overcome by fear and insecurity. They quit because they would rather leave now that they are ahead, than to face rejection; and they say no to everything because they are quick to imagine themselves at their downfall. Are you this type of person?

It may be a long process but it is possible to increase your self-worth you just have to really want to do it in the first place. If you are wanting to because you want to be successful start by learning to live a simple life, this may not make sense to you right now, but if you are really hungry for success, you should learn how to live simply. You do not have to be over complicated to be able to reach the top. Sometimes, you just have to do the right things. Always say, if you can think it, then it is almost yours. If you do not allow yourself to think of success, therefore, then you will never ever get there. Think of success, like it is already yours. Do not limit yourself to the little things.

You might not realize this but you should also learn how to recognize between good and bad beliefs. Some people are too overpowered by their beliefs that they are ruled by it. They do not realize that they are being limited by them, so it is important for you to have a way to look at things out of the box and from a distance. Embrace the positive that you can see. You have to know and understand how powerful it is. Negative thoughts have the ability to destroy dreams; but positive thoughts can invigorate even the weakest of people.

Learn how to embrace the positive because this will do you good; and learn how to get rid of the other things.

Beliefs→Thoughts→Feelings→Actions = Results.

To create empowering beliefs that improve your self-esteem, seek to become someone you admire—that is, do the kinds of things you admire in other people. What we admire in other people, we will also admire in ourselves. So for example, if we see ourselves being courageous, taking chances, or taking control of our lives, we start liking ourselves a whole lot more. All it requires is implementing some practices on a regular basis.

Here are ways to boost your self-esteem, so you feel empowered to take actions that advance your life and career:

> It's when we take 100% responsibility for our lives that life truly begins. Don't blame others for your circumstances. Make conscious choices. Decide what you want and how to get there, find solutions for any obstacles, and be the architect of the design for your life.

> Break down your biggest goals into smaller baby steps, complete one step at a time. Seeing yourself accomplishing tasks boosts how you will feel about yourself. At the same time, every step is a victory because you're moving forward.

Big successes come from many tiny victories.

Proving to yourself that you can step up and handle problems in your life proves to yourself that you are able to handle anything that comes your way. Fix your problems and feel proud of yourself for doing so.

Life begins outside your comfort zone, as the saying goes. It means being willing to be uncomfortable in order to achieve your goals. Even if you do find that you fail the first time you try, you will feel much more courageous and able to give it another go until you get it right.

Many people believe they're not worthy of happiness, plenty of people are living happy, fulfilled lives every day; some of them beyond age 100. How can you be one of them if you're always expecting the worst, you can begin removing that thought process form your brain by visualizing the best outcome in your mind, feeling it and expecting it. The more you do this the more of a shift you should experience.

*BE the person you strive to be and your life will follow you there.*

From Me Too You

*Dear reader, I am welcoming you to a part of my soul I haven't been able to open for a very long time with great efforts I tried but I was fearful of how much emotion and hurt I would have to purge from my soul for people to be able to relate to me. That fear no longer exists and I know how important it is for people to read about heartbreak, loss and healing too. We all tend to feel so alone when we are going through bad events in our lives so I hope that my collection of short stories, poems and quotes will make you feel comforted in times of despair, give you hope when you cannot find any and help when you really need it.*

Monophobia

*The worst nightmare was the one that kept me up all night, while he gave his soul to empty bodies in clubs, taking numbers of women making my heart feel numb, calling over and over in hope he was coming home, my fear of lonely had me sleeping alone.*

Love; A euphoric feeling, like being on a rollercoaster that you never want to end.

Clowning around

A collection of faces sat on my dressing table,

Clowning around with my different emotions,

Rouge red stained sadness lined with lies,

Maybelline black mascara and a contoured disguise,

I couldn't expose what lies beneath,
An endangered truth of the natural me,

I picked my face every day.

Clowning around, letting depression have its wicked way.

Time Machine

I felt like everything before that day was meaningless, waiting for calls that never made their way to my incoming call list,
Apologies that never left their lips,
Empty '' I love you's '' drowning in an abyss.

I felt re-born.
Sat writing poetry about all that I missed, realising happiness was on top of my wish list, Expressing emotions from lips newly un-kissed.

I am in my happy place as I am writing you this.

No matter how many times you have felt rock bottom beneath your feet or how many people picked you up and dropped you back down again, a diamond cannot be broken. You cannot be broken. Remember even when the sun isn't shining in your direction, you still shine regardless.

You are a diamond dear and don't you forget it.

S.H.E

She was my Sunday morning coffee,

Saturday night Hennessey,

Everyday necessity.

*You're the type of woman that love poems do not define,*

*you come into lives and change the unknown.*

*Men write love songs about you. the type wishing, they had never mistreated,*

*You deserve an undoubting love, spoiled with packages full of loyalty,*

*Don't settle where you do not know where you stand.*

That's the beauty of crying, even roses need some water to bloom so don't dwell on the reason just grow through the season.

[ Please forgive yourself for the mistakes you made. If you did not go through what you went through, you would not know what you know now. Everything works together for the greater good when you are on your path to purpose. Trust your journey.]

The pain that you feel could never compare to the happiness that is coming your way.

Time, Words & Energy.

Three things you can never get back once exchanged, choose wisely.

*'' She designed a life for herself that she loved''*

She is brave enough to go to war for everything that she wants, a savage for everything she knows she deserves. The wild hearted woman who never settles where there is no truth. They say she is like a wildfire; so beautiful to watch but so hard to put out.

*'' What is the point in mastering a language if you don't say what you feel''*

And suddenly she knew that she deserved more than the bullshit she had settled for, the season changed and so did her mind. She stopped needed them to love her and realised how her tree blossomed when she began to love herself.

I knocked knowing she was in pieces,
She didn't come with 'how to care 'instructions,
Or a guide on fixing her back together, Chaos
was all she had ever known, Misguided by a
broken home.
Wrapping her in my arms, I told her that her heart was no
longer on temporary lease,
I treated her like my most valuable masterpiece.

'' Maybe nobody ever took the time out of their day to let you know that you are beautiful, five minutes to tell you that you are worthy. A second of their day to smile when you feel so sad. That is okay, as long as you know you are beautiful, you are worthy and whenever you feel sad I care for you so please don't give up''.

*Happiness is simply doing what you love.*

Her.

She wasn't like the rest of the world; it was in the way she carried herself.

She knew that even though she had made mistakes she was imperfectly flawed and all of her dreams unfolded before her eyes every time she told herself '' *I believe in you* ''.

She didn't need a man to motivate her, she was motivation enough for herself. That doesn't mean life was easy but it certainly was a challenge she was willing to win.

And whenever you saw her she was never on social media or out in the clubs, she sat at home with a book in her and wine in the other, laughing at the thought of a no-good man ever trying to love her.

Be the woman who makes him believe in fairy-tales.

*Maybe we are so used to being hurt by people who claim to love us that we no longer know the difference between a person who loves us and a person who just say's that they do.*

There is something beautiful about the woman who does not beg for attention,

The woman who does not need likes on social media to like herself,

You know the pretty woman with the good energy who like's hood music and Hennessey.

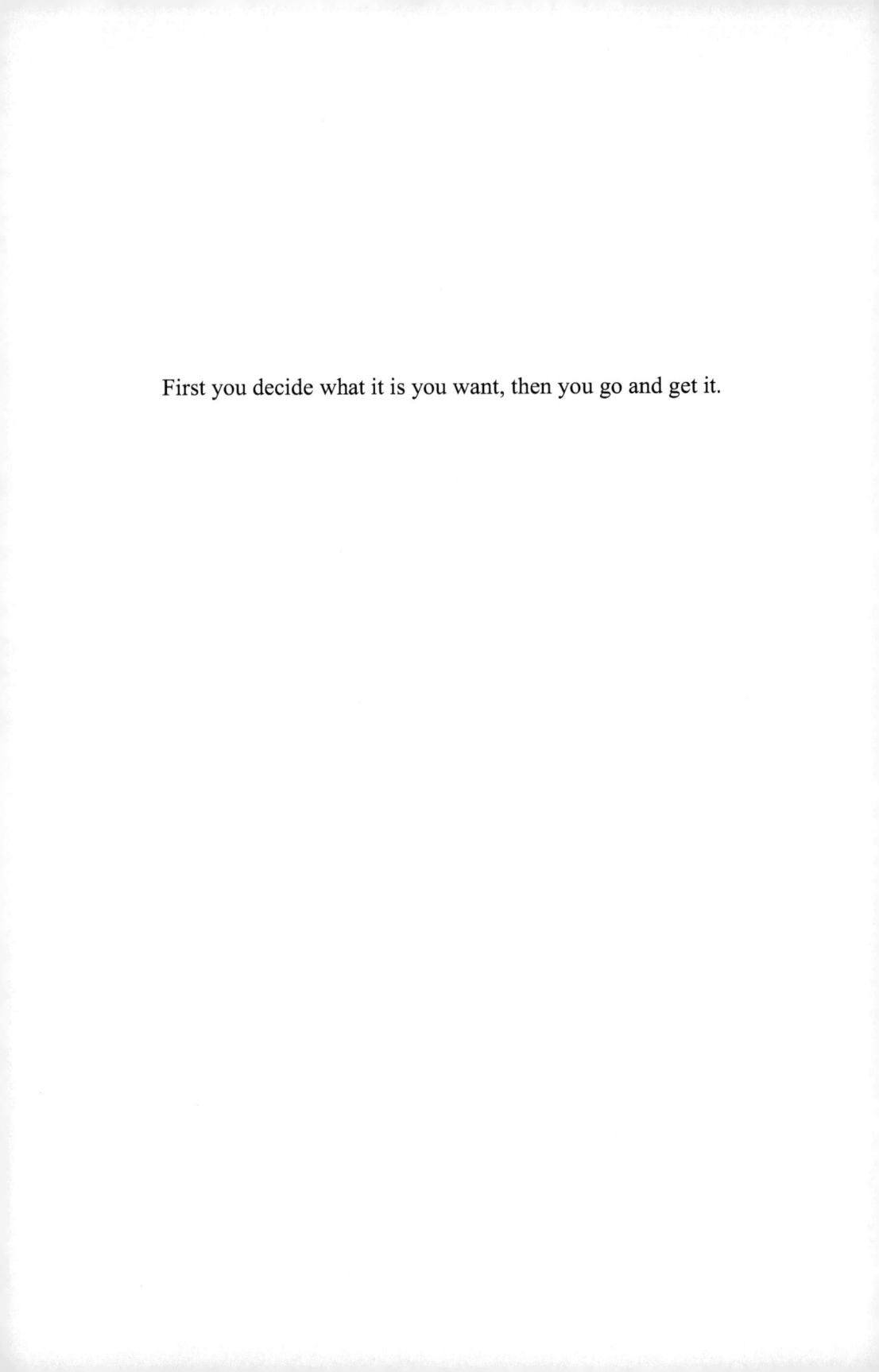

First you decide what it is you want, then you go and get it.

Success is never a straight line from start to finish, it is moments you wish you never started and day's you are so happy that you did.

You will always be enough but never be enough for the wrong person. Go ahead and place yourself in the hands of a real man/woman and watch how much you elevate.

She Laughed.

'' I never lost him, he lost me. Now he will spend the rest of his life searching for me in every single woman that he meets not knowing that he will never find it again.''

Be who you are not what they say.

The dangerous women are the ones who refuse to let a man shade her in war because she is always equipped to win.

That's the thing about being a good person, you never stop searching for good in every bad person that you meet.

Create a dream board and use it to visualise everything that you want to achieve, include your dream car even your dream wedding if that's what you want. Give yourself something to work towards.

Stop worrying about what if you don't succeed and focus on that fact that you CAN.

Not everyone will applaud you.

Not everyone will stand beside you and support you.

And please don't expect people to care.

But applaud yourself,

Support yourself,

Care for yourself,

You are all that you have in this world, focus on that and let that be enough motivation for you to do anything you want to.

A broken heart: Paralysis and body numbing throughout.

You will never find your soulmate if you have not become a master of your own soul yet, everyone you meet will abuse the fact you don't even know how amazing you are.

*People change and then they grow. Its normal and it's okay for them to grow away from you and you grow away from them, if we never grow we never get anywhere new.*

You know on the days you really feel like throwing the towel in and giving up? Ask yourself if you don't wake up tomorrow was it worth spending all of today feeling defeated?

POSITIVE ENERGY

STAY POSITIVE

Darkness

A great immensity came from her thrill of watching the sun set over shards of glass shattered across her floor, a picture of him lying in the shadows.
- She laughed.

'' Now you know how it feels to be left in the darkness by the person who promised you light ''

All of your dreams start with the idea that you can achieve them first, remember everything that you think is everything that you will become.

'' Abuse isn't always physical. Sometimes a person can abuse your mind, your being, the way you feel towards them. Be aware of that, just because they aren't smacking you in the face doesn't always mean they aren't abusing your love.''

When you find a king, keep him.

When you find a queen, value and protect her.
Don't re-shuffle the deck then complain when you end up with a joker.

Remember, it doesn't matter how much you think he like's you because he doesn't like you that much if you are still waiting for him to text you back.

    Persistence is key.

It's not selfish to choose to love yourself, it's the right thing to do when you have things in your life that you want to achieve. Spending all your time loving them won't leave room for you to supply the love you deserve.

Anyone can get up and go to work to make money and pay their bills but not everyone can handle the sacrifices involved in chasing a dream that requires you to do things you have never had to do before. Not everyone can handle the amount of stress involved in being hungry for success and always wanting more, some people are content and some people never are.

The obstacles and issues you encounter are placed to test you not destroy you, I just want you to know that you should never give up. You don't get the credit you deserve until you make it but I want you to know you are valuable and your efforts to get to where you want to be are going to be the same things that get you there, and beyond.

Keep going.

There's good women then there's bad bitches like there's good mothers and useless ones. We choose who we have in our lives like we choose who mothers our children, people will find arguments against it but that is exactly what it is. Don't complain when the bad bitch you choose starts to act like a dog, it was a choice you made. Good women have nice breasts and big bums too they just choose not to focus on them as their only blessings. It's always about the decisions we make and the understanding behind them, men if you want good don't try to find that in someone who is really stupid enough to call themselves a bitch in the first place.

It really doesn't matter about who you used to be all that matters is who you are choosing to become.

Love smells so much better when the right person wears it.

The Devil at my door

He kept knocking when he wanted, dressed in all black

Looking through my windows finding the chair where he once sat

Pointing that he will claim it and he will have it back

I never dared to move a muscle in case he saw I was in
How many times did I have to tell him I no longer want to sin?

He lived here once and burned it down

I started from scratch and I don't want him now.

When you choose to look at what you already have in life, you will always have enough.


If you look at what you don't have, what you do have will never be enough.

*'' There is no price on a good woman''*

Your life begins at the roots you plant for yourself, when you choose to dig deeper no matter how many rocks get in your way, you choose to create the life you deserve despite how many setbacks try to deny you of that right. The most beautiful flowers are the ones whose roots are embedded in strong soil.


Grow baby.

*Walking alone can be the hardest but it will always make you the strongest.*

- Don't expect to find your happiness within people who are so happy with being less than you was promised.

True loneliness is trying to fill empty spaces with empty people who have no intentions of pouring purpose and happiness into our lives.

Let go

Pray

Accept

Cleanse

Repeat

*Buried deep within the stained tears on her cheeks, lays a story of how she survived moments in her life that she thought would be the death of her. You see rivers of black mascara flowing; she could tell you how she feels years of pain being released.*

Sometimes the devil comes dressed in everything you thought you ever wanted and tells you all the things you thought you needed to hear. Then takes it all away with no warning or preparation.

While you are reading these words

Wishing you had all the answers to your problems

Praying for happiness and good luck

I really want you to know that it is all going to be okay.

You are so worthy of this life

You are so deserving of the happiness you wish for

I will never stop praying for every sad person to find the peace they need. You are a survivor

Keep surviving.

The final goodbye

Life.

A word with so much meaning yet so difficult to understand, we have no choice over it we are given it and have to learn what we can do to make the best out of it. Some people are lucky enough to be born into a very happy one and others not so lucky, either way we all hit a point in our life that we feel we want more, we need more or we want to be more and it can be very hard working out how we are supposed to do that. I decided to share these parts of my life and my soul with you in hope they will play a part in making it even slightly easier for you, I don't know if they ever will but I truly hope you know that I have wrote to you with the best of intentions. I pray endlessly that everyone reading this is granted the eternal happiness you all deserve.

> Never give up creating the life that you want no matter how hard it gets, you are stronger than you will probably ever know, more beautiful than you will ever see and you are capable of achieving anything you believe that you can.
>
> I believe in you and I want you to always keep going.
>
> Keysha

Printed in Great Britain
by Amazon